beyond your number

an enneagram journal
to guide you forward
with greater wholeness

Type 8

Stephanie J Spencer

Certified Enneagram Coach

stephaniejspencer.com

with special thanks to

Ashley M Leusink
for graphic design and layout support
find out about her work as a spiritual director at
jesusandgin.com

Rachel McCauley
for copyediting support
find out about her work at
linkedin.com/in/rachel-d-mccauley

this journal is dedicated to

my family
who supports me, laughs with me, loves me,
and has been patient with me in the messy process
of finding my way as an enneagram coach.

my friends
who nerd out with me in enneagram conversations,
help me stay grounded and connected,
and remind me of the power of human belonging.

my clients
who teach me what it is to live as their enneagram types,
and give me wisdom to pass along
to others in my work.

Dear Reader,

Enneagram is not a personality test. It is a tool that gives insight into who we are and why we do what we do. These insights are intended to help us move forward in wholeness, freeing us from the passions and fixations of our types.

But knowing how to break out of these confines can prove difficult. We read books, listen to podcasts, follow Instagram accounts, and are left with the question, "Now what?"

The work can be daunting. This journal is meant to guide you through the forward movement of enneagram.

Its questions are designed to open space for you to see your behaviors, motivations, fears, and hopes with more clarity and compassion. The more honest we are with ourselves, the more insight we have into what practices might help us move forward in wholeness.

Growth is more like a wide and rocky river to navigate than a narrow set of steps to climb. Two people who are the same enneagram type may need to focus on vastly different areas of change. Our paths toward greater wholeness will be as diverse and unique as our backgrounds. Therefore, this journal is meant to be worked through as a winding path, taking you where you believe you need to go. It is not a fixed path from Point A to Point B.

The place where one person begins could be an ending place for another. The work you have already done might be the work someone else needs to begin.

I hope you will look through this journal, and allow questions to "rise from the page." The question that sticks out to you now is the one to sit with today. Answer it. Let a new question rise off the page when you are ready. Go at your own pace. Stay with a question as long as necessary: a day, a week, or a month. There isn't a right or a wrong pace.

However you engage with this journal, I hope it helps you on your journey of becoming the best version of you.

In hope,
Stephanie

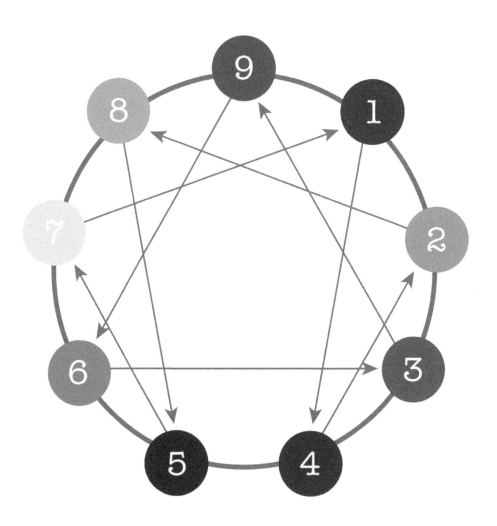

an enneagram overview

Enneagram is a framework that gives us insight into nine primary ways people engage in the human experience. These nine numbers are the enneagram types. The symbol that holds these numbers is a visual picture of the energy and interaction of the types. It is a framework that holds both complexity and unity, allowing us to be both a lot like other people and uniquely ourselves.

The circle reminds us we are all connected. We hold and display all numbers to some extent. However, we rest in one number as our home-base.

Our home-base enneagram type is the lens through which we see and experience the world.

When we know our type, we find language for the underlying factors that motivate us. We think about things like what we are afraid of, what we desire, and what makes us feel vulnerable. Knowing our enneagram number helps us name our shadows with compassion and take steps to live more deeply into our gifts.

No enneagram type is better or worse than another type. This is why numbers are more helpful than titles. As soon as we add words, there are things we do and don't want to be.

All nine enneagram types carry important facets of what it means to be human.

Each type is more of a spectrum than a point. We draw on the numbers next to our type as well, often drawing on one more strongly than the other. These adjacent numbers are called our wings.

Numbers connected to us by lines reflect our movement toward other types. In stressful states, we move with the arrow, compelled toward behaving like that type. In relaxed or secure states, we move against the arrow, opening to receiving the energy of the other type moving toward us.

Our enneagram number and its connected points are all important parts of who we are. We need to learn how to move in and receive the energies of each of them in order to move forward in wholeness.

recommended resources

This guided journal is meant to be a resource for those who already know their enneagram type and are familiar with the system. If enneagram is new to you, or you want to learn more, here are some places to explore.

websites

integrative9.com

enneagraminstitute.com

drdaviddaniels.com

podcasts

The 27 Subtypes of the Enneagram by The Liturgists

Typology with Ian Morgan Cron

The Enneagram Journey by Suzanne Stabile

music

Atlas: Enneagram by Sleeping at Last

primers

Enneagram Spectrum of Personality Styles by Jerome Wagner

The Road Back to You by Ian Morgan Cron and Suzanne Stabile

Enneagram Magazine Issue #1

deeper dives

The Complete Enneagram by Beatrice Chestnut

The Enneagram in Love and Work by Helen Palmer

The Sacred Enneagram by Chris Heuertz

The Wisdom of the Enneagram by Don Riso and Russ Hudson

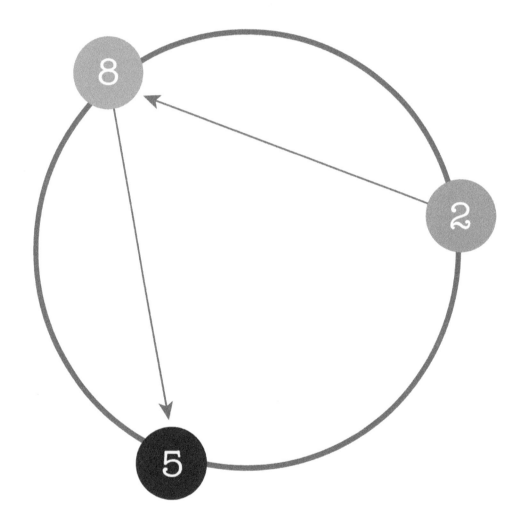

an overview of Type 8

Enneagram Type 8s intuitively sense where power resides in others and in themselves. They are naturally assertive, independent, and decisive, but can sometimes lean towards being proud, domineering, or confrontational. Type 8s are sensitive to justice and protective of the underdog. They do not like to be vulnerable, which can create an exaggerated need to be control. Type 8s have a drive to conquer that carries a strong energy.

As they pause to engage with their heads and hearts, Type 8s display the virtue of innocence, which allows them to connect to the present moment without expectations or prejudgments. This helps them carry a magnanimous presence and leadership.

When Type 8s feel stress, they connect with the energy of Type 5, which can look like objectivity, detachment, or hoarding.

When Type 8s feel secure, they connect with the energy of Type 2, which can look like possessiveness, nurturing, or compassion.

why orange?

Orange is a strong and lively color. Its attention grabbing and visible nature is ideal to represent the energy of Type 8s. Orange is not a color that sits in the shadows: it is a color that creates shadows.

Orange is used as a color for many sports teams, as it carries a winning energy. Orange is also a protective color used for traffic cones and high visibility clothing.

Orange can be overwhelming. Like the fruit bearing the same name, its flavor can be strong. Type 8s may need to remember that they can cause a strong reaction in others.

Type 8s are part of the Assertive Triad, matched in brightness by the colors of Type 3 (red) and Type 7 (yellow) on the enneagram symbol. These three types are the most independent and energetic. They want to take charge of their environments.

When Type 8s feel secure, they access the green of Type 2. This combination can be a reminder of autumn, a season when orange is connected to coolness and acceptance of the natural rhythms of life and death on the earth.

May what I do flow from me like a river, no forcing and no holding back, the way it is with children.

Rainer Maria Rilke

Enneagram is a map and a guide.
It does not describe the entire geography of the human landscape. It is meant to help us grow in awareness and move towards health and wholeness. It is not intended to hold every nuance and attribute of a human person.
I am an enneagram type.
I am ALSO a unique individual.

In what ways does enneagram Type 8 describe me?

In what ways does enneagram Type 8
not describe me?

How can I keep the tensions between my uniqueness
and enneagram Type 8 in mind as I do this work?

Are there any potential barriers keeping me from
doing the work of the enneagram?

Can I remove some of these barriers
before diving deeper?

What resources do I need in order to engage in the work of the enneagram? (i.e. intentional time)

Are there concrete supports that would help me move forward? (i.e. a friend with whom to process)

What is making me feel vulnerable, defensive, or afraid right now?

Do any of these things need to be resolved before moving forward with this journal?

Can I look at my habits with compassion
and choose to change them to reflect the values
true to my essence?

What might keep me from seeing myself with hope,
possessing the potential for change?

Can I use the enneagram as a tool to become more embodied and present to my life and relationships?

Can I keep this posture and goal in mind as I keep moving forward?

Are there ways I am trapped within
my enneagram type?

How do I need to recognize the transformation I have
already done before beginning the work of this
journal?

words that can be used to describe Type 8

decisive   no nonsense   empowering

risk-taking   tough   assertive

limit-pushing   dominant   territorial

protective   direct   possessive

fair   tough   capable

leader   domineering   defender

forceful   hardworking   denying

charismatic   fearless   intimidating

unrefined   magnanimous   confident

blunt   revolutionary   strong

What are three words I like?

What are three words I don't like?

What are three words that once
described me but no longer do?

What are three words that describe me now?

Not everything that is faced
can be changed,
but nothing can be changed
until it is faced.

James A. Baldwin

on strength

Do I feel the need to protect people?
Why? How?

Are those I want to protect in need
of my protection?

How has life told me I need to be strong?

Could I get more comfortable with weakness?

Am I aware of the impact my voice and presence has on others?

Is there a time recently when someone else might have needed more space than I provided?

When I have been defensive?
When have I been aggressive?

What might it feel like to soften my approach to others?

Do I hold back from showing fear,
vulnerability, sadness, or affection? Why?

What might happen if I revealed
my heart more often?

How has my determination propelled things forward that might have stalled out without my work and advocacy?

Is the intensity with which I push obtrusive to those around me?

How has my "all in" mentality served me well?
How has it hurt me?

Where and when am I driven towards excess?

What problems has this caused in my life?

Am I open to broad forms of relational connection?

Do I value my relationships with people who carry
a lower level of intensity than me?

Am I in touch with my dependency on others?
Why? Why not?

How would it feel to accept help or support
more often?

on independence

Where am I looking to control the people or environment around me?

What would it look like to trust more?

Have I been impatient with inaction in ways that have moved things forward too quickly for my own good?

When has my self-sufficient energy allowed me to work hard and long for the benefit of myself and others?

What would happen if I let go of pushing things forward and allowed more situations to take their natural course?

How has my straightforward directness served me well in relationships?

The small man

Builds cages for everyone

He

Knows.

While the sage,

Who has to duck his head

When the moon is low,

Keeps dropping keys all night long

For the

Beautiful

Rowdy

Prisoners.

Hafiz

on justice

How has my concern for justice brought
good into the world?

When has it turned from a hope for justice
into a desire for vindication?

How do I respond when I witness powerlessness or unfair treatment of myself or others?

In what areas is my community better because I have used my voice and authority on their behalf?

When have I been compelled to take matters into my hands that were not actually under my authority?

When was this a helpful choice?
When was this an unhelpful choice?

Are there issues I frame as being about justice that could actually be about something else?

How often am I assuming others have good intentions?

How often am I assuming others have negative or unjust intentions?

When have I failed to see the middle ground?

How might the situation have been
different if I had?

Have I made a caricature of someone who has disappointed me?

If I worked to see more from his/her point of view, might my opinion change?

How am I expecting those around me to
"hold their own" in conflict with me?

Is this expectation fair?

When have I expanded my presence to fill the space I perceived as a void?

When did this serve me? When did this serve the group?

When did this cause pain?
When has this kept people from being seen and heard?

How do I see strength valued and reflected in my life?

When has my desire to assert authority
been helpful?

When would others or myself have been better
served by me not taking the driver's seat?

Yesterday I was clever,
so I wanted to change the
world. Today I am wise,
so I am changing myself.

Rumi

Our first response to stress tends to be
to "double down" in our primary type.

In higher levels of stress, Type 8 moves toward Type 5.
The movement can be unhealthy or healthy,
paralyzing or resourcing.

Words that might describe a Type 5 include
detached, scholarly, precise, curious, reclusive, analytical, hoarding,
specialized, pedantic, inventive, secretive, prudent, Intellectual,
independent, perceptive, objective, pithy

When I feel stress, do I become controlling, get decisive, push
limits, or display other stereotypical traits of Type 8?

Are there times when stress has made me feel like
a "different person"?

In stress, am I slipping into the less healthy
characteristics of Type 5 and

... pulling my energy inward and turning anger on myself?

... retreating into emptiness, isolation,
or intellectual spiraling?

... feeling my intensity combine with a sense of grabbing,
in fear of not having enough?

In stress, am I connecting with the healthier characteristics of a Type 5 and

... gaining the patience of thinking longer before acting?

... finding space to reflect and observe?

... connecting my gut to my head in ways that increase my compassion and objectivity?

Integrating my inner Type 5 will help me move forward in wholeness.

Can I consciously open myself to the healthier characteristics of this type?

When I feel secure, I may feel or act differently than I do at other times, and even from the typical descriptions of my enneagram type.

In security, Type 8 moves toward Type 2.
The movement can be unhealthy or healthy, paralyzing or resourcing.

Words that might describe a Type 2 include sacrificing, repressing, intuitive, compassionate, intrusive, listening, flattering, generous, possessive, hospitable, rescuing, nurturing, controlling, manipulative, gentle

Some people might feel secure on a day off, or on vacation, or at home, or with a trusted friend.

What helps me feel secure?

In security, am I slipping into the less healthy characteristics of a Type 2 and

... using assistance as a way to keep people dependent upon me?

... looking to others to affirm my strength?

... manipulating others to affirm my worth?

In security, when am I connecting with the
healthier characteristics of a Type 2, and...

... connecting my desire for justice with a heart for
mercy and care?

... using my energy and confidence to build community and
empower others?

... becoming more gentle and tender in my interactions
with others?

**Integrating my inner Type 2 will help
me move forward with wholeness.**

Can I consciously open myself to the healthier
characteristics of this type?

You know that the antidote to exhaustion is not necessarily rest? ... The antidote to exhaustion is wholeheartedness.

David Whyte

How have I cultivated my presence to come out from behind a wall with a receptivity to tenderness and wonder?

Are others experiencing the virtue of innocence emanating from my heart?

How is my bighearted toughness offering care and protection to others?

How am I letting go of control and aligning with the flow of reality?

Am I coming to each moment without expectations or prejudgments?

How am I combining autonomy and empathy with justice and mercy to empower others with gentleness?

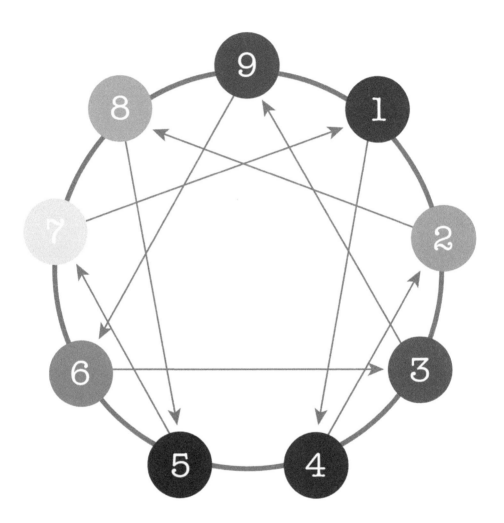

now what?

The question at the beginning of this journal re-surfaces. You have read books, listened to podcasts, perused websites, and followed Instagram accounts. Additionally, you have worked through this journal. I hope what you've written here will continue to be a reference that leads you to better, more complete versions of yourself.

But the question remains... now what?

Keep moving forward. It takes continual work to stay aware of ourselves. This world has a tendency to lull us to sleep.

Actively keep the characteristics, habits, and passions of your Type in your mind as you move through daily choices. Celebrate ways you have grown and notice where you still have room to move forward.

Take time to learn about numbers other than your own. Notice ways other Types exist in some way within you. If there is work to do there, open yourself up to it. (This may be especially useful with your stress response and security numbers.)

Ask the people in your life about their Types, and notice the similarities and differences in how you experience the world. Use enneagram as a tool to help you grow in compassion towards others.

Breathe. Be. Stay in touch with your body. Ground your questions with presence.

You may want to keep this journal to look at once or twice a year. Notice how your answers change. Celebrate the journey.

And if you get discouraged, maybe you can take with you one of my favorite quotes, from Parker Palmer,

"What a long time it can take to become the person you've always been."

From one becomer to another,
Stephanie

CPSIA information can be obtained
at www.ICGtesting.com
Printed in the USA
LVHW071956031120
670479LV00005BA/144